FANTASTIC SPORT FACTS

RUGBY

Michael Hurley

Raintree

Raintree is an imprint of Capstone Global Library Limited, a company incorporated in England and Wales having its registered office at 7 Pilgrim Street, London, EC4V 6LB – Registered company number: 6695582

www.raintreepublishers.co.uk
myorders@raintreepublishers.co.uk

Text © Capstone Global Library Limited 2013
First published in hardback in 2013
First published in paperback in 2014
The moral rights of the proprietor have been asserted.

Edited by Catherine Veitch, Sian Smith,
  and John-Paul Wilkins
Designed by Richard Parker
Picture research by Ruth Blair
Originated by Capstone Global Library Ltd
Printed and bound in China

ISBN 978 1 406 25350 4 (hardback)
16 15 14 13 12
10 9 8 7 6 5 4 3 2 1

ISBN 978 1 406 25356 6 (paperback)
17 16 15 14
10 9 8 7 6 5 4 3 2

British Library Cataloguing in Publication Data
Hurley, Michael.
Rugby. -- (Fantastic sport facts)
796.3'33-dc23
A full catalogue record for this book is available from the British Library.

Acknowledgements
We would like to thank the following for permission to reproduce photographs: Corbis p. 24 (© Dimitri Iundt/TempSport); Getty Images pp. 7 (Ben Hoskins/Stringer), 8 (Matt Turner/ALLSPORT), 9, 21 (David Rogers), 17 (GABRIEL BOUYS/AFP), 19 (Mark Kolbe), 23, 25 (David Rogers /Allsport), 27 (Bob Thomas); PA Photos pp. 26 (Press Association Images), 11, 20; Photoshot pp. 5 (© Xinhua), 22 (© Offside/Talking); Shutterstock pp. 6 (© Neil Balderson), 12 (© kosam), 13 thermometer (© Oleksiy Mark), 13 dog (© Eric Isselée), 14 (© Eoghan McNally); Superstock p. 16 (© Marka).

Cover photograph of Jonny Wilkinson reproduced with permission of Getty Images (ANNE-CHRISTINE POUJOULAT/AFP), and a rugby ball reproduced with permission of Shutterstock (© RTimages).

Every effort has been made to contact copyright holders of any material reproduced in this book. Any omissions will be rectified in subsequent printings if notice is given to the publisher.

Contents

Some words are printed in bold, **like this**. You can find out what they mean by looking in the glossary.

Rugby basics

The two most popular types of rugby are Rugby Union and Rugby League. The main difference between the two is the number of players. In Union there are 15 players, while League has 13.

This map shows the main rugby playing **nations.**

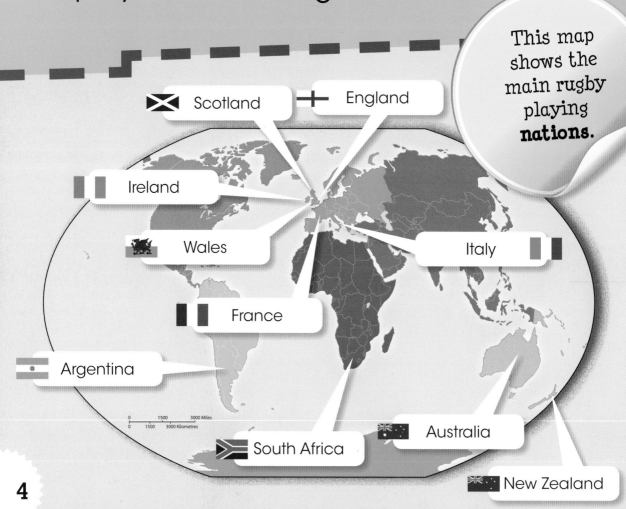

Scotland

England

Ireland

Wales

Italy

France

Argentina

0   1500   3000 Miles
0   1500   3000 Kilometres

South Africa

Australia

New Zealand

DID YOU KNOW?

The biggest rugby union competition is the World Cup. This is held every four years.

New Zealand won the World Cup in 2011.

First ever game

The first rugby union international game took place in 1871. The match was played between Scotland and England. Scotland won.

England and Scotland have played each other more than 130 times.

A **try** is so called because originally when a player carried the ball over the line they were allowed to "try" to kick a goal to score points.

Big crowds

One of the largest crowds at a rugby match – 109,874 fans – watched Australia play New Zealand in Sydney in 2000.

New Zealand won the match 39 - 35.

DID YOU KNOW?

A large crowd attended a charity match between teams of famous players from the northern and southern **hemispheres** in 2011.

Highest-scoring game

The record for the highest score by a rugby union team was set by Hong Kong in 1994. They beat Singapore 164 – 13. This game also set the record for the highest total number of points in one game, with 177.

HONG KONG	164
SINGAPORE	13

RECORD BREAKERS

Ashley Billington scored a world record 50 points (10 **tries**) in the match.

Unusual matches

A match between Samoa and Fiji in 1924 was played on a pitch with a tree growing in the middle! The game started at 7.00 a.m. because the Samoa players had to go to work afterwards!

WOOF!

When Portsmouth Victoria played the Southampton Trojans in 1886, the ball bounced off a stray dog at the edge of the pitch. A Portsmouth player grabbed the ball and scored. The Trojans **protested**, but the try was allowed to stand!

FUN FACT

In Russia, a rugby match was once played at -23 degrees Celsius! This is the coldest game ever recorded.

50
40
30
20
10
0   0
10
20
30
40
50

°C

Super scrum!

The **scrum** is one of the most powerful things in sport. During a scrum, a **pack** can create up to 1.4 tonnes of force. That's a lot of pushing power!

RECORD BREAKERS

In 2012, a group of children from Belfast broke the world record for the largest scrum. There were 840 children in the scrum!

The Haka

One of the most famous and entertaining sights at a rugby match is the Haka. The New Zealand team does this traditional Maori dance before every game. The Haka can strike fear into the **opposition**.

DID YOU KNOW?

Before the final of the 2011 Rugby World Cup, France responded to the New Zealand Haka by linking arms. They showed that they were not afraid.

Biggest rugby ball

The world's biggest rugby ball was made in Hong Kong. It is 4.7 metres long and 2.95 metres high. That is bigger than a car!

The ball was created to celebrate the Hong Kong **Sevens** rugby **tournament**.

The Hong Kong Sevens tournament attracts the best teams in the world.

Tallest and shortest

The tallest ever rugby player is Richard Metcalfe. The former Scottish international is 2 metres and 13 centimetres tall.

FUN FACT

The shortest rugby player on record is Namibia's Riaan Jantjes. He is just 1 metre and 52 centimetres tall.

Winger Jason Robinson was selected twice for the **British and Irish Lions.**

DID YOU KNOW?

Tall, powerful players are usually **defensive** players. Shorter, faster players usually play on the **wing.**

Kicking for glory

Former England **fly-half** Jonny Wilkinson kicked the winning points in the 2003 Rugby World Cup final. Wilkinson uses a special **technique** to help him kick accurately.

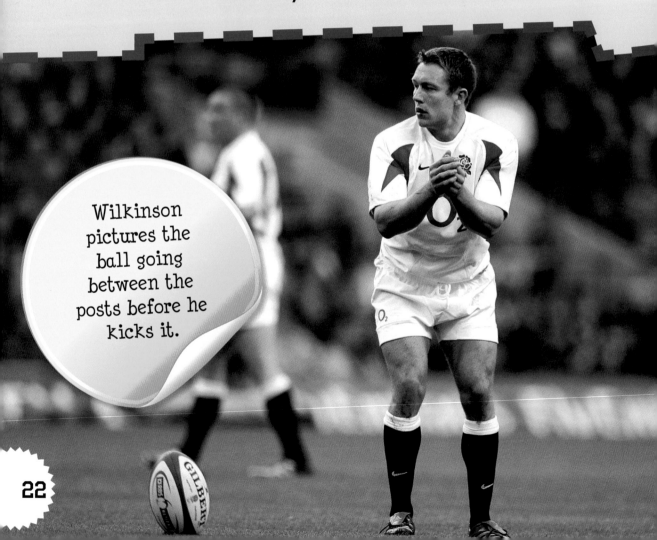

Wilkinson pictures the ball going between the posts before he kicks it.

DID YOU KNOW?

Michael Lynagh played fly-half for Australia for 11 years. He is the highest points scorer in Australian rugby, with 911.

Outstanding players

STATS

Height: 1.96 metres

Weight: 120 kilograms

International caps: 60

International tries: 37

New Zealand rugby legend Jonah Lomu is one of the greatest players of all time. He could run the 100 metres in just 10.8 seconds!

David Campese is the all-time leading **try** scorer for Australia, with 64 tries in 101 matches.

The star of women's rugby is England's Maggie Alphonsi. She played in the final of the 2010 Women's Rugby World Cup.

DID YOU KNOW?

Martin Offiah is a rugby league legend. He scored 501 **tries** during his career.

Quiz

Are you a superfan or a couch potato? Decide whether the statements below are true or false. Then look at the answers on page 31 and check your score on the fanometer.

1 New Zealand have won the World Cup more than any other country.

2 The Argentina national rugby team is known as the Pumas.

3 The record for the highest number of points scored in one match was set in 1994.

4 Rugby balls were originally made out of pig bladders.

5 Johnny Wilkinson kicked the winning points in the 2003 Rugby World Cup final.

6 David Campese played 100 times for Australia.

FANOMETER

couch potato

all-rounder

superfan

1   2   3   4   5   6

Glossary

British and Irish Lions rugby union team made up of players from England, Scotland, Ireland and Wales

defensive used as a defence

fly-half rugby player who plays in the middle of the field and directs play

hemisphere either of two halves of Earth. The northern and southern hemispheres are divided by an imaginary line called the equator.

nation country made up of people who share the same language and culture

opposition person or team being competed against

pack group of forwards in a rugby team, who gather together to form a scrum

protest show that you disagree with something

scrum way of beginning play in rugby when the opposing packs form together with their heads down and push against each other

Sevens faster, shorter version of rugby. Each team has only seven players.

technique special way of doing something

tournament competition where there is a series of games or contests

try act of touching the ball down over the goal line

wing left or right side of a rugby pitch

Find out more

Books

Rugby (Inside Sport), Clive Gifford (Wayland, 2010)

World Rugby Records 2012, Chris Hawkes (Carlton Books Ltd, 2011)

Websites

pbskids.org/kws/sports
Find out more about your favourites sports, including tips on how to play.

www.rugby.com.au/tryrugby/ KidsRugby/KidsFunZone/ OnlineGames.aspx
Play online interactive rugby games here.

Quiz answers

1) False. Australia, New Zealand, and South Africa have all won two World Cups.
2) True.
3) True. The teams scored 177 points in total (see page 10).
4) True.
5) True (see page 22).
6) False. David Campese played 101 times for Australia (see page 25).

Index